Let's Investigate Plants!

I0866280

Plants Have Many Parts!

By Ruth Owen

KidHaven Publishing

Published in 2024 by
KidHaven Publishing, an Imprint of Greenhaven Publishing, LLC
2544 Clinton St., Buffalo, NY 14224

Copyright © 2024 by The Rosen Publishing Group, Inc.

Portions of this work were originally authored by Ruth Owen and published as *What Do Roots, Stems, Leaves, and Flowers Do?*
All new material this edition authored by Ruth Owen.

Produced for Rosen by Ruby Tuesday Books Ltd
Editor for Ruby Tuesday Books Ltd: Mark J. Sachner
US Editor: Designer: Emma Randall

Photo Credits:
Cover, 4–5, 6–7, 9, 10 (right), 11, 12, 14, 16, 17 (top), 18–19, 20–21, 22–23, 24, 25 (bottom), 26–27 © Shutterstock; 8, 28–29 © Ruby Tuesday Books; 10 (left) © Superstock; 13 © Istockphoto; 15 © FLPA; 17 (bottom) © Science Photo Library; 25 (top), 25 (center) © Wikipedia Public Domain.

Cataloging-in-Publication Data

Names: Owen, Ruth.
Title: Plants have many parts! / Ruth Owen.
Description: Buffalo, New York : KidHaven Publishing, 2024. | Series: Let's investigate plants! | Includes glossary and index.
Identifiers: ISBN 9781534545694 (pbk.) | ISBN 9781534545700 (library bound) | ISBN 9781534545717 (ebook)
Subjects: LCSH: Plants--Juvenile literature. | Roots (Botany)--Juvenile literature. | Stems (Botany)--Juvenile literature. | Leaves--Juvenile literature. | Flowers--Juvenile literature.
Classification: LCC QK49.O94 2024 | DDC 580--dc23

All rights reserved.
No part of this book may be reproduced in any form without permission in writing from the publisher, except by a reviewer.

Manufactured in the United States of America

CPSIA compliance information: Batch #CSKH24: For further information contact Greenhaven Publishing LLC at 1-844-317-7404.

Please visit our website, www.greenhavenpublishing.com.
For a free color catalog of all our high-quality books, call toll free 1-844-317-7404 or fax 1-844-317-7405.

Find us on

Contents

Tiny and Tall

A tiny, colorful pansy may grow to just a few inches high, while a giant sequoia tree can be taller than a 20-story building.

It's hard to imagine that these two living things are in any way the same, but they are both plants. Scientists estimate there are almost 400,000 different **species** of plants on Earth!

Whether tiny or giant, most plants have the same parts—roots, stems, and leaves. Many types of plants also have flowers. Together, these plant parts work together to help a plant grow, stay healthy, and even produce future plants.

Roots in Action

Most plants have roots that grow down into the soil.

The roots of some plants spread out horizontally in the soil. Trees usually have this type of root. A large tree may have woody roots as thick as a person's arm. Thinner, hairlike roots grow from the thick roots.

Other plants have one main root that grows down into the ground. This long, thick root is called a **taproot**. Dandelions and carrot plants have taproots. The orange carrots we eat are actually the thick taproots of carrot plants.

In order to be healthy, plants need water and **nutrients**, such as nitrogen, potassium, and calcium. A plant's roots act like drinking straws, taking in water and nutrients from the soil. The nutrients are dissolved in water so the plant can use them.

Standing Up Strong

A plant's roots also have another important job. They must give the plant stability and keep it standing upright in the soil.

Without roots, most plants would topple over when the wind blows or as their branches, leaves, or flowers grow and became heavy. The roots of a large tree may spread underground in an area two or three times the diameter of the tree's branches. Many trees survive for years on steep slopes because their roots hold the trees steady in the soil.

This tree lives on a steep slope and has been blown sideways by the wind. Its roots still hold it in place!

A dandelion is also a good example of how roots can anchor a plant in soil. Try tugging one of these little plants out of the ground, and you will likely end up with only a handful of leaves and stems. The dandelion's taproot will stay firmly underground!

Stems for Support

The stems of a plant may have many different names—including trunks, branches, or twigs—but they all do the same jobs and form a framework that supports the plant.

Thinner stems grow from a plant's main stem and connect to its leaves or flowers. On a tree, stems that grow from the plant's main stem (or trunk) are known as branches. The branches connect to even thinner stems, called twigs, where the leaves grow.

A plant's stems contain a system of tubes called **xylem** and **phloem**. The xylem tubes carry water and nutrients from the roots through the plant's stems to its leaves. A plant's leaves act like little factories that make food for the plant. The phloem tubes carry this food from the leaves to wherever it is needed inside the plant.

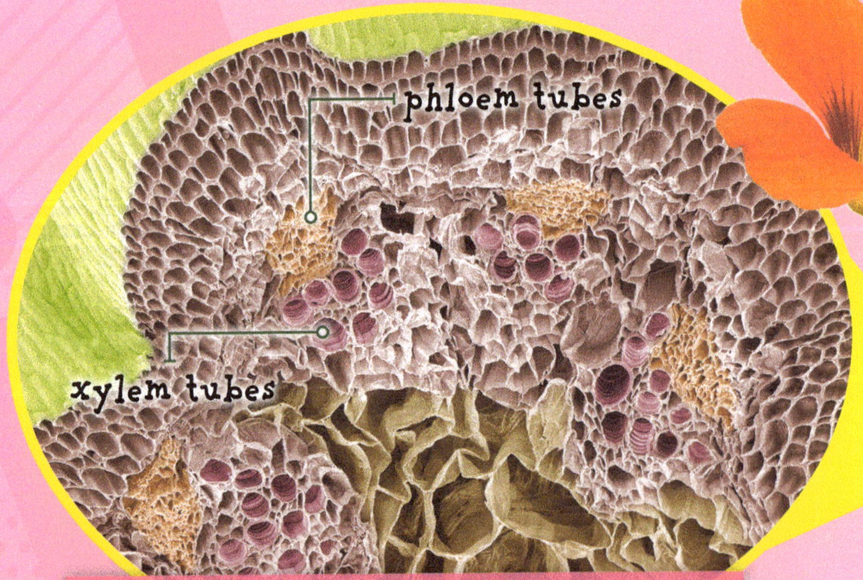

This image was taken by a scanning electron microscope. It shows a slice from a nasturtium stem that has been magnified about 100 times.

a twig and leaves from a tree
a framework of branches
a tree's stem, or trunk

Super Stems

Some plants are record-breaking giants, and it's usually their stems that make them the superstars of the plant kingdom.

A giant redwood tree in Redwood National Park in California is currently the tallest tree on Earth. The record-breaking tree, named Hyperion, has grown to almost 381 feet (116 m) tall. That's over 70 feet (21 m) taller than the Statue of Liberty! It's possible, however, that one day an even taller tree might be discovered.

The 2,000-year-old Tule tree in Santa María del Tule, Mexico, has one of the thickest trunks on Earth. In fact, it looks as if it's several trunks joined together. The tree's trunk measures 119 feet (36 m) around.

Bamboo is a type of thick-stemmed grass plant from Asia. The stems of one species of giant bamboo can grow up to 3 feet (1 m) in a single day!

Giant bamboo is a fast-growing, huge species of grass.

What Do Leaves Do?

The leaves on a plant—whether big, small, long, spiky, or shiny—have a very important job to do. They make food for the plant.

A plant may take in nutrients from the soil, but that's like you taking vitamins. To grow and remain healthy, you also need proper meals to give you energy. A plant is the same. It needs a type of sugary food for energy. It makes this food inside its leaves using water, **carbon dioxide** from the air, and sunlight.

The leaves of some plants are smaller than a dime. Others are enormous, like the leaves of the gunnera plant (also called giant rhubarb), which can grow to more than 10 feet (3 m) across.

a gunnera, or giant rhubarb, plant

The Leaves Get Cooking

The process of making food inside a plant's leaves is called photosynthesis.

Photosynthesis takes place with the help of a substance called **chlorophyll**. It's the chlorophyll in plants that gives them their green color.

The chlorophyll in a plant's leaves traps the energy in sunlight. Water is delivered to the leaves from the roots. The leaves take in carbon dioxide from the air through **microscopic** holes called **stomata**. Once the ingredients are in place, a plant's leaves use sunlight to turn the water and carbon dioxide into a sugary plant food.

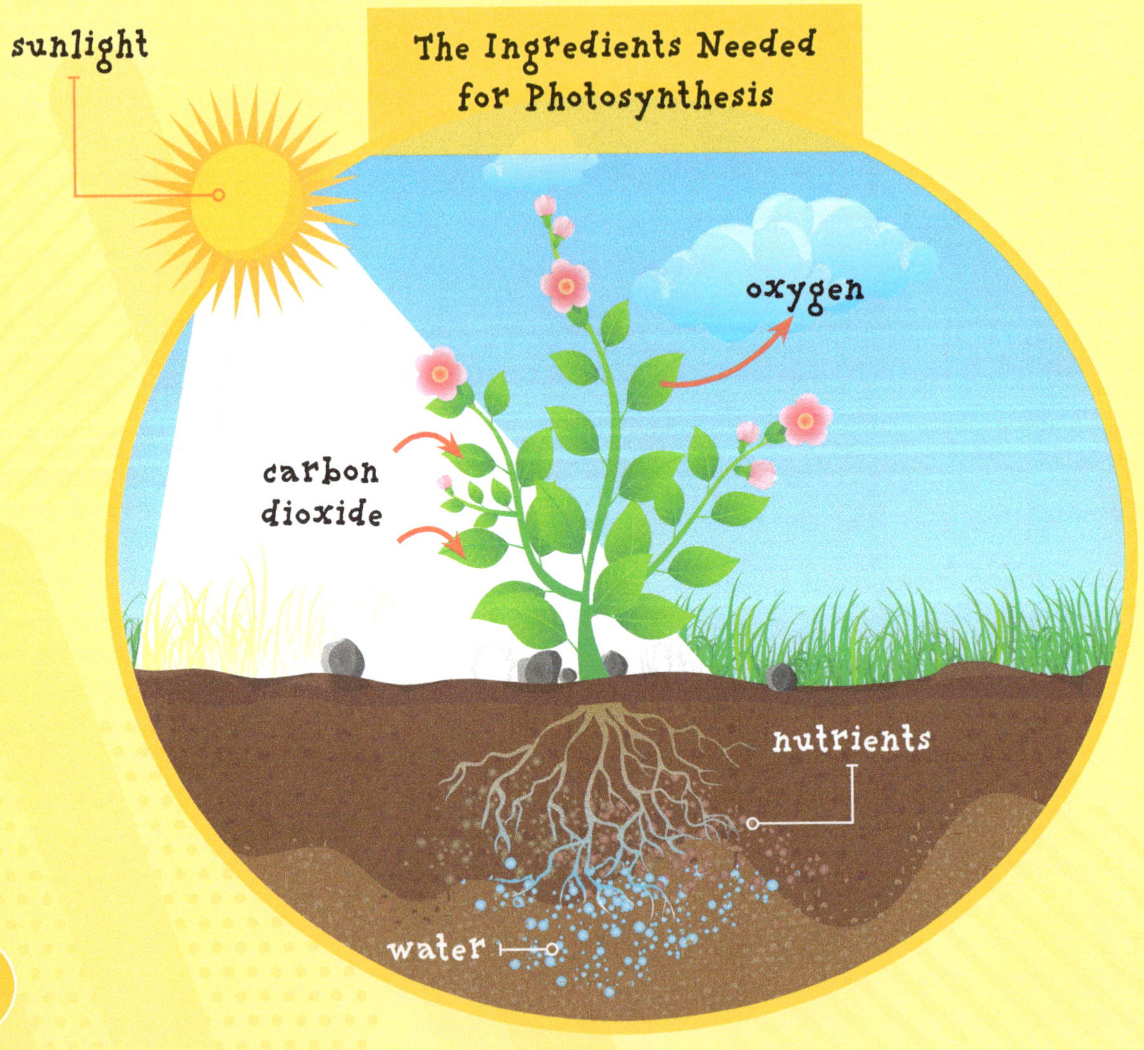

During photosynthesis, something else important happens. Plants make oxygen and release it from the stomata in their leaves. Without plants, humans and other animals would have no oxygen to breathe!

stomata on a potato plant leaf, as seen under a microscope

A Winter Rest

In the fall, many tree leaves turn yellow, brown, orange, or red. Then they fall to the ground. Why does this happen if trees need their leaves to make food?

During winter, the days are short, with few hours of sunlight. There is often less rain in winter, too, and water in the soil may freeze. With little sunlight and water available, a tree's leaves cannot make enough food to feed the tree. Growing and keeping leaves healthy uses a lot of energy, too. So, in readiness for the tough winter months, many trees drop their leaves in the fall. The tree then stops growing and rests until spring to save energy.

When a tree's leaves stop making food, they also stop making green chlorophyll. This allows the leaves' other colors, which are normally hidden by green, to show through.

Stay Green, Save Energy

Some trees live in tough habitats where sunlight and water are in short supply all year round. These trees are called coniferous, or evergreen, trees.

The leaves of many types of coniferous trees look like thin, green needles. These trees don't drop all their leaves in autumn. Instead, they lose and regrow small quantities of leaves all year long.

Just like the leaves of other plants, each needle-like leaf on an evergreen tree is able to make food for the tree using water, carbon dioxide, and sunlight. Having leaves all year allows coniferous trees to make food whenever they get the chance.

Also, growing a whole new set of leaves each spring uses up a lot of energy. Therefore, tough coniferous trees hold onto their leaves and save energy!

Each thin pine needle shown here is a leaf.

coniferous trees
growing on rocks

What Does a Flower Do?

Flowers look beautiful and often smell great, but they have a very important job to do. They make seeds, which allow plants to **reproduce**.

Flowers produce a dust called **pollen** on their anthers. The pollen from one flower, such as a lily, must be carried to the **stigma** of another lily. The lily with pollen on its stigma is now **pollinated** and is ready to begin making seeds.

Some flowers are pollinated by the wind blowing their pollen from flower to flower. Other flowers need help from animals such as insects, birds, and bats. When an animal, such as a butterfly, lands on a flower, some pollen sticks to its body. Then the butterfly flies off and visits a different flower of the same kind. Some of the pollen on the butterfly's body brushes off and sticks to that flower's stigma.

a butterfly pollinating a lily flower

How Seeds Grow

Once a flower has been pollinated, seeds begin to develop. The seeds form inside plant parts that protect them as they grow.

For example, a poppy plant's seeds grow inside a hard, hollow case called a seedpod. The seeds of an apple tree grow inside protective fruits that we know as apples. In time, the plant's flowers die, leaving only the fruit or seedpod behind.

1

poppy flower

a seedpod forming

2

fully formed poppy seedpods

3

poppy seeds

split seedpod

Once the seeds are fully grown, a seedpod will split open. The seeds fall to the ground, where they can grow into new plants. Apples and other fruits fall to the ground, too. Then the fruits rot away, allowing the seeds inside to settle on the soil, ready for growing.

A Seedling Grows

Seeds usually wait until spring to start growing. They may have fallen to the ground naturally or been planted in soil by a farmer or gardener.

First, roots grow from the seed into the soil. Next a seedling, or shoot, grows from the seed. Then tiny leaves sprout from the seedling. The seedling's roots and stems deliver water to the leaves. The young leaves take in carbon dioxide and use sunlight to begin making food for the plant.

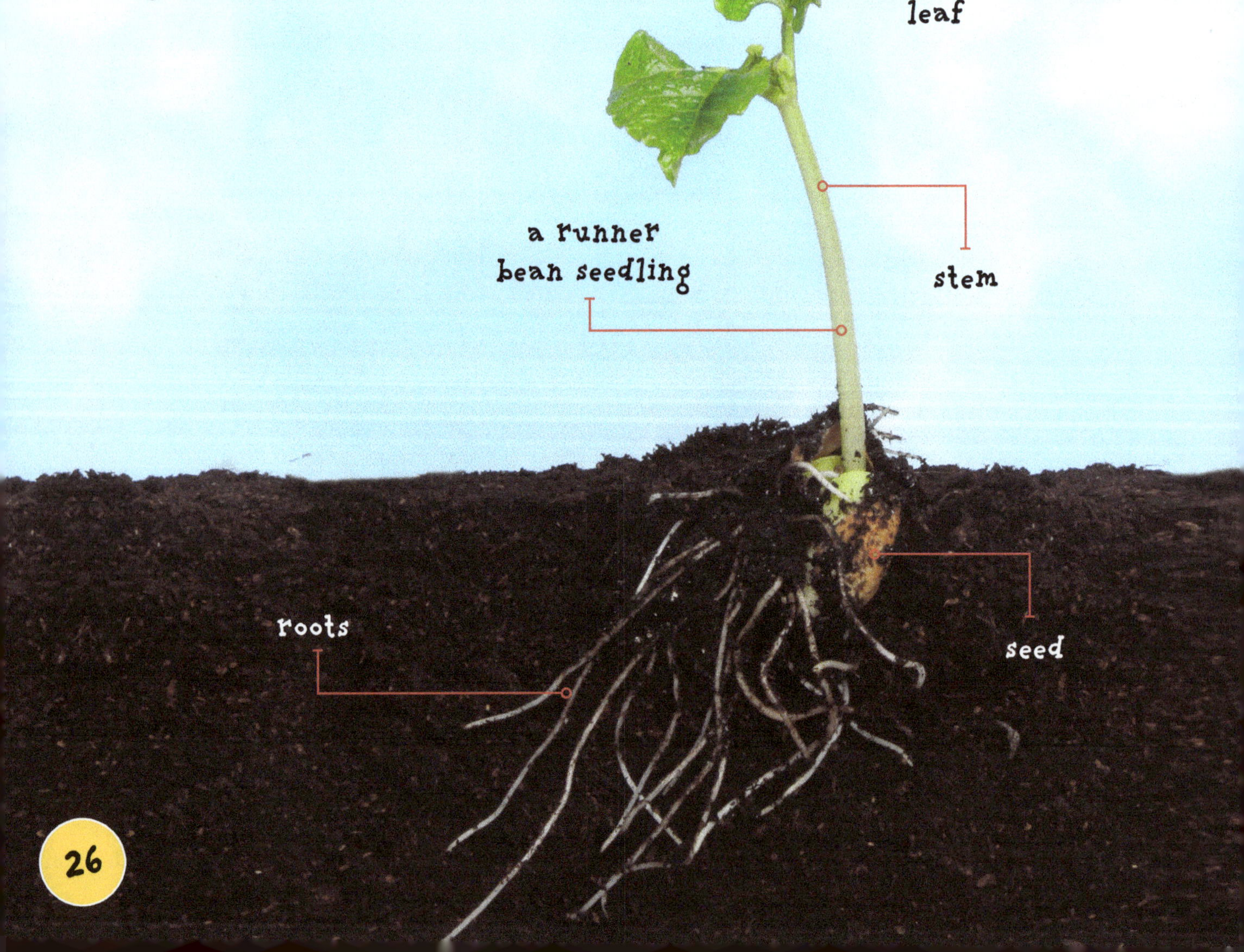

a runner bean plant with flowers

The new plant grows bigger and stronger. In time, if it's a flowering plant, it will grow flowers for making seeds. A runner bean plant may take just weeks to grow. A tree may take hundreds of years. However long its life, the different parts of a plant keep working together to help the plant grow, stay healthy, and reproduce.

People eat the seedpods of runner bean plants.

Let's Investigate Plant Parts

How do plant stems work?

Water and nutrients are delivered through a plant's stems inside thin tubes. How do we know this? Let's investigate!

YOU WILL NEED:

- water
- a glass
- a teaspoon
- blue food coloring
- a knife and cutting board
- a celery stalk with leaves

Step 1:
Put 1 inch (2.5 cm) of water into the glass.

Step 2:
Mix two teaspoons of blue food coloring into the water.

Step 3:
Using a knife, carefully cut 1 inch (2.5 cm) from the bottom of the celery stalk. *(Only use a knife if an adult is there to help you.)*

Step 4:
Stand the celery stalk in the blue water. Over the next few days, the celery stalk and leaves will turn a blue or bluish color.

Day 1

Day 3

Why? How? What?

Why do you think the celery stalk and leaves turned blue?

(See page 32 for the answer.)

How does a plant take in water?

The orange part of a carrot plant is actually its main root, or taproot. Does this mean the root can take in water and help the plant grow new leaves? Let's investigate!

YOU WILL NEED:

- a small glass
- water
- a carrot
- a knife and cutting board
- a wooden skewer

Step 1:
Fill the glass with water to about 0.5 inch (1.25 cm) from the top.

Step 2:
Cut about 1 inch (2.5 cm) from the top of the carrot. *(Only use a knife if an adult is there to help you.)*

Step 3:
Push the skewer through the carrot top and then balance the skewer on the top of the glass so the carrot is touching the water.

Step 4:
Put the glass in a sunny place. Top off and refresh the water in the glass every few days.

Step 5:
Within a few days, you'll see stems and leaves growing from the top of the piece of carrot root. Tiny threadlike roots may even begin sprouting from the piece of carrot.

Why? How? What?

How is the piece of carrot helping the new leaves grow?

(See page 32 for the answer.)

Glossary

carbon dioxide (KAHR-bun dy-OK-syd) A colorless gas in the air that plants use to make food. When humans and other animals breathe out, they release carbon dioxide into the air.

chlorophyll (KLOR-uh-fil) The substance that gives plants their green color. Leaves use chlorophyll for making food during photosynthesis.

coniferous (kah-NIH-fur-us) Referring to trees that often grow in cold, tough habitats and do not lose their leaves in winter. Many have needlelike leaves.

habitats (HA-buh-tats) Places where animals or plants normally live. A habitat may be a backyard, a forest, the ocean, or a mountainside.

microscopic (my-kreh-SKAH-pik) So small that an object can only be seen through a microscope and not with just a person's eyes alone.

nutrients (NOO-tree-ents) Substances needed by a plant or animal to help it live and grow. Plants take in nutrients from the soil using their roots. The nutrients in soil are dissolved in water.

phloem (FLOH-em) Tubes inside a plant that carry food from the leaves through the stems to wherever it is needed inside the plant.

photosynthesis (foh-toh-SIN-thuh-sus) The process by which plants make food in their leaves using water, carbon dioxide, and sunlight.

pollen (PAH-lin) A colored dust made on the anthers of flowers, which plants need in order to reproduce.

pollinated (PAH-luh-nayt-ed)
When pollen is carried from the anthers of one flower to the stigma of another. Some flowers need pollen from another flower of the same species in order to be pollinated. Other types of flowers are able to self-pollinate. This means pollen from the flower's anthers can be transferred to its own stigma.

reproduce (ree-pruh-DOOS)
To make more of something, such as when plants make seeds that will grow into new plants.

species (SPEE-sheez)
One type of living thing. The members of a species look alike and can reproduce together.

stability (stuh-BIH-luh-tee)
The ability to be stable, which in the case of a plant means standing upright and not falling over.

stomata (sto-MAH-tuh)
Microscopic holes on a leaf that a plant uses for taking in carbon dioxide and releasing oxygen.

taproot (TAP-root)
A thick main root of a plant that grows down into the soil. Often, some thin, hair-like roots grow from a taproot.

xylem (ZI-lum)
Tubes inside a plant that carry water from the roots, through the stems, and to the leaves.

Websites

https://www.nhm.ac.uk/discover/plants.html

https://photosynthesiseducation.com/photosynthesis-for-kids/

https://www.fs.usda.gov/managing-land/wildflowers/pollinators/what-is-pollination

Read More

Bolte, Mari. *How Plants Will Save the World (STEM to the Rescue)*. Minneapolis, MN: Full Tilt Press, 2023.

Newland, Sonya. *Plants (Outdoor Science)*. Mankato, MN: Capstone Press, 2020.

Owen, Ruth. *Roots, Stems, Leaves, and Flowers (Get Started with STEM)*. Minneapolis, MN: Ruby Tuesday Books, 2017.

Index

Answers

Page 28
The xylem tubes in the celery stalks carried the blue water through the stalks and up to the leaves, dyeing them blue. You can see the tubes as tiny blue dots in the stalk if you cut them.

Page 29
The piece of carrot taproot is taking in water just as the root would if it were in soil. Having water and sunlight allows the carrot plant to start growing new leaves.